TIME FOR
TEA

BOOK

WATFORD, UK

Tea With Friends

A JOY WORTH REPEATING,
AGAIN AND AGAIN,
WARM CONVERSATION, TEA,
AND A FRIEND.

MISS MADELINE

There is something undeniably
heartwarming and conversation-making
in a cup of steaming hot tea.... It is an
ideal prescription for banishing
loneliness. Perhaps it is not so much
the tea itself, as the circle of happy
friends eager for a pleasant chat.

BOOK OF ETIQUETTE

ADDICTS

Water is the world's most
common drink,
followed, of course, by tea.

HELEN THOMSON, b.1943

Tea is my panacea, my consolation –
if you will, my "fix".

DIANA KENNEDY

The perfect way to start the day
is with a cup of tea in bed.
The perfect way to end the day is
with a cup of tea in bed.

STUART AND LINDA MACFARLANE

One sits on the bus, rain trickling
off one's nose, shoes saturated,
feet aching –
and thinks longingly of a cup of tea.

PAM BROWN, b.1928

[I am] a hardened and shameless
tea-drinker who has for many years
diluted his meals with only the infusion
of this fascinating plant; whose kettle
has scarcely had time to cool;
who with tea amuses the evening,
with tea solaces the midnight,
and with tea welcomes the morning.

SAMUEL JOHNSON (1709-1784)
DRANK 40 CUPS PER DAY

THE REWARDS OF TEA

Tea tempers the spirits and harmonizes
the mind, dispels lassitude and
relieves fatigue, awakens thought
and prevents drowsiness, lightens
or refreshes the body, and clears
the perceptive faculties.

CONFUCIUS (551-479 B.C.)

[Tea makes you] feel wiser, braver and
more optimistic after drinking it.

GEORGE ORWELL,
FROM "A NICE CUP OF TEA"

Peter Fiore, USA

"THE TEA STORY"

... very seldom do we go through a day without drinking, thinking, reading or hearing about tea. And that is true of almost every country in the world whatever may be the race, creed, or politics of its inhabitants. Tea is in the office and the factory, the train, the aeroplane. It is on the high mountains, in the bush or forest, on the sea and under it. It is drunk from eggshell cups of translucent porcelain and mugs of earthenware; from the most expensive china, from a cup of jade in a golden saucer such as was offered to Père Huc, and from chipped old military mugs. It is in the palace, the country house, the suburban semi-detached and the cottage of the labourer. Essentially, classlessly, it belongs to every home. It is the form of hospitality which can be offered by the rich to the poor or the poor to the rich, equally and without embarrassment on either side. It celebrates domestic happiness and soothes the nerves of failure or fatigue.

J.M.SCOTT, FROM "THE TEA STORY"

TEA JUST FOR TWO

TWO PEOPLE SITTING OVER A POT OF TEA
AND HOT BUTTERED TEACAKES
PUSH ALL THE HUGE INTERNATIONAL ANXIETIES
TO THE EDGES OF PERCEPTION –
AND LIVE FOR A LITTLE WHILE
IN AN EDEN OF THEIR OWN.

PAM BROWN, b.1928

TEA IN TIMBUCTOO

Nearly 3,000 feet up a mountain
in Wales. Misty, bitterly cold, desolate.
Heavens above! Man inside hut brewing
and selling hot, strong Indian tea.
Thick cups, no saucers. What nectar!

MRS IVY POTTS

There is only one thing worse
than cheap tea – and that is to serve it
with evaporated milk.
Unless you have just done a four hour
watch at sea –
when it tastes like nectar.

PAM BROWN, b.1928

In some thirty years of travelling
the dusty roads of India [I] have found
tea in its many manifestations a cheerful
and invigorating travelling companion,
a companion I can't do without.

SHERPA TENZING

Nobody who has not travelled in the East
and arrived, after a day's tramp through
a malarious and steaming jungle, at some
poor Chinaman's shanty, and thankfully
drunk a dozen cups of the beverage,
freely offered, can know how delicious
and invigorating even the most modest
tea can be.

HENRY NORMAN, FROM "THE FAR EAST"

A WARM WELCOME

The cup of tea on arrival
at a country house
is a thing which, as a rule,
I particularly enjoy.
I like the crackling logs,
the shaded lights, the scent
of buttered toast, the general
atmosphere of leisured
cosiness.

P.G. WODEHOUSE
(1881-1975)

WE LOVE OUR TEA

Whether in clinking bone-china
in leisured drawing-rooms or chunky
mugs on building sites, we love
our tea. It comforts us and gently
stimulates and makes us feel at home.
Less neurotic than coffee, less sticky
than squash, less problematical than
alcohol, it goes well with real life:
with cake, and sympathy, and
moments of undemanding
companionship.

LIBBY PURVES

If you are cold tea will warm you –
if you are heated, it will cool you –
if you are depressed, it will cheer you –
if you are excited, it will calm you.

WILLIAM E. GLADSTONE (1809-1898)

It's the stirring of tea that makes the
world go round.

STUART AND LINDA MACFARLANE
SELF-CONFESSED TEA FANATICS

A. E. Marty, 1931

OUR STOMACH WILLS IT...

is very strange, this domination of our intellect
by our digestive organs. We cannot work,
we cannot think, unless our stomach wills so.
It dictates to us our emotions, our passions....
After a cup of tea (two spoonfuls for each cup,
and don't let it stand for more than three
minutes), it says to the brain, "Now rise, and
show your strength. Be eloquent, and deep,
and tender; see, with a clear eye, into Nature,
and into life: spread your white wings of
quivering thought, and soar, a god-like spirit,
over the whirling world beneath you,
up through long lanes of flaming stars to
the gates of eternity!

JEROME K. JEROME (1859-1927),
FROM "THREE MEN IN A BOAT"

"IT MAKETH THE BODY ACTIVE AND LUSTY"

It maketh the Body active and lusty.
It helpeth the Head-ach, giddiness and
heaviness thereof.
It removeth the Obstructions of the Spleen.
It is very good against the Stone and Gravel,
cleansing the Kidneys and Uriters being drunk
with Virgin's Honey instead of sugar.
It taketh away the difficulty of breathing,
opening Obstructions.
It is good against Lipitude, Distillations,
and cleareth the sight.
It removeth Lassitude, and cleareth and
purifieth adult Humors and a hot Liver.

It vanquisheth heavy Dreams, easeth the Brain, and strengtheneth the Memory.
It overcometh superfluous Sleep, and prevents Sleepiness in general, a draught of the Infusion being taken, so that without trouble whole nights may be spent in study without hurt to the Body.
It prevents and cures Agues, Surfets, and Feavers, by infusing a fit quantity of the Leaf, thereby provoking a most gentle Vomit and breathing of the Pores.

THOMAS GARWAY,
FROM A BROADSHEET IN 1660, ADVERTISING TEA

THE TEA HOUR

As an institution [the tea hour] is kindly,
as an incident it is stimulating. It conveys
at one end the same time a sense of tradition
and a sense of intimacy.

AGNES REPPLIER (1855-1950),
FROM "TO THINK OF TEA"

There are few hours in life more agreeable
than the hour dedicated to the ceremony
known as afternoon tea.

HENRY JAMES (1843-1916)

A DELIGHT

Tea, thou sober, sage and venerable
liquid, thou... tongue running,
smile soothing, heart opening,
wink tippling cordial to whose
glorious insipidity I owe
the happiest moments of my life,
let me fall prostrate.

COLLEY CIBBER (1671-1757)

Come, oh come, ye tea-thirsty
restless ones – the kettle boils,
bubbles and sings, musically.

RABINDRANATH TAGORE (1861-1941)

... tea is not simply a staple,
like salt or oatmeal, but also
a delight – a trip – even a
revelation now and then!

JAMES NORWOOD PRATT,
FROM "THE TEA LOVER'S TREASURY"

K. Hokusai, Japan

TEA IS A WORK OF ART

Tea is a work of art and needs a master
hand to bring out its noblest qualities...
There is no single recipe for making
the perfect tea, as there are no rules for
producing a Titian or a Sesson.

Each preparation of the leaves has its
individuality, its special affinity with
water and heat, its hereditary memories
to recall, its own method of telling a
story. The truly beautiful must be always

in it. How much do we not suffer
through the constant failure of society
to recognize this simple and
fundamental law of art and life....

KAKUZO OKAKURA (1862-1913)

Bringing Harmony and Balance To Life

Socially, the ritual of the tea break
is part of the fabric of our society.
Putting the kettle on
for a cup of tea
is reassuring, especially at times
of great pressure and stress,
we do it automatically.
At work it gives us the opportunity
to have a gossip
which should be encouraged
because communicating is good for us.

DR. DAVID LEWIS

Tea is mankind's oldest established
and most loved beverage
because a cup of tea is good to the taste
and because it makes life more pleasant
by the feeling of well-being
that it gives to mind and body.

GERVAS HUXLEY, FROM "TALKING OF TEA"

Tea tempers the spirit and harmonizes
the mind; dispels lassitude and relieves fatigue;
awakens thought and prevents drowsiness;
lightens and refreshes the body and clears
the perceptive faculties.

LU YU, FROM "CH'A CHING (THE CLASSIC OF TEA)"

THE GOOD LIFE

One cup in the morning will set
the spirit stirring, refreshed, and
bring the opening of untapped
thoughts;
one cup of tea after a meal will
clear mouth odours and drive
worries away;
one cup of tea when you are
busy will quench your thirst,
drive care away and render a

feeling of tranquility;
one cup of tea after your day
is done will make your bones and
muscles fell lighter and dissolve
your fatigue;
tea will drive the doctor away, and
make you feel strong;
tea will add to your years, and the
enjoyment of your longevity.

ANCIENT CHINESE POET

... THE REAL WEALTH OF THE TEA TABLE

LIES IN ITS ABILITY TO ENRICH THE EVERYDAY,

GILD THE MOMENT WITH IMPORTANCE,

AND CELEBRATE THE LOOSENING

OF THE DAY'S DEMANDS.

CATHERINE CALVERT, FROM "HAVING TEA"

Walter Osborne Ireland

whose plot was woven about the tea,
the flowers, and the paintings.
Not a color to disturb the tone of the room,
not a sound to mar the rhythm of things,
not a gesture to obtrude on the harmony,
not a word to break the unity of
the surroundings, all movements
to be performed simply and naturally –
such were the aims of the tea ceremony.

KAKUZO OKAKURA (1862-1913)

Toulouse-Lautrec

Tea With Grandma

Any connoisseur will confirm
that the excellence of a tea depends
principally upon its place of origin.
A recent survey shows that in
ascending order of merit these are:
from a vending machine, from a
train buffet, at a top restaraunt,
at a friend's house, at home,
at Gran's.

STUART AND LINDA MACFARLANE

PROPER MOMENTS FOR DRINKING TEA

When one's heart and hands are idle.
Tired after reading poetry.
When one's thoughts are disturbed.
Listening to songs and ditties.
When a song is completed.
Shut up at one's home looking over paintings.
Engaged in conversation deep at night.
Before a bright window and a clean desk.
With charming friends and slender concubines.
Returning from a visit with friends.
When the day is clear and the breeze is mild.
On a day of light showers.
In a painted boat near a small wooden bridge.

In a forest with tall bamboos.
In a pavilion overlooking lotus flowers
on a summer day.
Having lighted incense in a small studio.
After a feast is over and the guests are gone.
When children are at schools.
In a quiet, secluded temple.
Near famous springs and quaint rocks.

HSÜ TS'ESHU, FROM "CH'ASU"

ZEST – A GENTLE HIGH

Drink tea that your mind may be lively and clear.

During our ascent [of Everest]
Indian tea constantly gave us
cheer and vigour.

A large part of the pleasure tea affords
is that it gets you high.... It is a high so gentle
that we seldom notice either lift or letdown,
yet it is for the sake of this high that the drink
has been developed and constantly refined by
generations of tea lovers over the centuries.
Tea increases mental alertness and agility,
brightens the spirits, sharpens sensations,
and enhances intellectual discrimination.

JAMES NORWOOD PRATT,
FROM "THE TEA LOVERS TREASURY"

52

It (being prepared and drank with Milk
and Water) strengtheneth the inward parts,
and prevents consumption, and powerfully
assuageth the pains of the Bowels, or griping
of the Guts or Looseness.
It is good for Colds, Dropsies and Scurveys,
if properly infused purging the Blood
of Sweat and Urine, and expelleth Infection.
It driveth away all pains in the Collick
proceeding from Wind, and purgeth
safely the Gall.

THOMAS GARWAY,
FROM A BROADSHEET IN 1660, ADVERTISING TEA

SURVIVING WITHOUT TEA

What would the world do without tea?
How did it exist?
I'm glad I was not born before tea!

SYDNEY SMITH (1771-1845)

Withdraw the tea-break
and the economy collapses.

PAM BROWN, b.1928

We haven't had any tea for a week....
The bottom is out of the universe.

RUDYARD KIPLING (1865-1936)

The most heartfelt cry
of the returning shopper is
"I could murder a cup of tea".

PAM BROWN, b.1928

It's not true that drinking tea is
habit-forming. Even after drinking twenty
cups a day for forty years it would still be
as easy to give up tea as it would be to give
up breathing.

STUART AND LINDA MACFARLANE

For me any tea, even a tea-bag doused in
tepid water, is better than no tea.

SHERPA TENZING

56

Ignace Fantin-Latour, 1864

CRISIS! DISASTER!

In labour or semi-concious on a stretcher,
saved from the sea or rescued from a mountain –
"Do you think I could have a cup of tea?"

PAM BROWN, b.1928

The Police, the Medical Profession, Welfare
workers, Firemen – all know two vital things
how to deliver a baby – and how to make
a cup of tea.

CHARLOTTE GRAY

Peace, Quiet, Calm...

When I drink tea,
I am conscious of peace.
The cool breath of Heaven
rises in my sleeves,
and blows my cares away.

LU T'UNG,
CHINESE POET OF THE T'ANG DYNASTY, c.700

One drinks tea
to forget the world's noise;
it is not for those who eat rich food
and dress in silk pyjamas.

T'IEN YIHING, c.1570

Drinking tea, eating rice,
I pass my time as it comes;
Looking down the stream,
Looking up at the mountain,
How serene and relaxed I feel indeed!

PAO-TZU WEN-CH'I

In Sad Times

What part of confidante has that poor
teapot played ever since the kindly plant
was introduced among us.
Why myriads of women have cried
over it, to be sure! What sickbeds it has
smoked by! What fevered lips have
received refreshment from it!

WILLIAM MAKEPEACE THACKERAY
(1811-1863), FROM "PENDENNIS"

You can taste and feel, but not describe,
the exquisite state of repose produced
by tea, the precious drink which drives
away the five causes of sorrow.

CHI'EN LUNG
CHINESE EMPEROR
(RULED FROM 1735-1795)

THE SEVENTH CUP...

The first cup moistens my lips and throat, the second cup breaks my loneliness, the third cup searches my barren entrail but to find therein some five thousand volumes of odd ideographs. The fourth cup raises a slight perspiration – all the wrong of life passes away through my pores. At the fifth cup I am purified; the sixth cup calls me to the realms of the immortals.

The seventh cup –
ah, but I could take no more! I only
feel the breath of cool wind that rises
in my sleeves....
Let me ride on this sweet breeze
and waft away thither.

LU T'UNG,
CHINESE POET,
OF THE T'ANG DYNASTY, c.700

STRENGTH AND PURPOSE

One cup taken and enjoyed, one refreshing sip
and all the differences of opinion, even hostility
cease. A headache vanishes. Courage returns.

AUTHOR UNKNOWN, FROM GRACE/SUMMER 98

Every good cause and every generous object
gains strength, and purpose, and determination
when it is heated over a cup of tea.

JAMES HURNARD

65

Dale Kennington, USA

Strangely enough humanity has so far met

in the teacup. It is the only Asiatic

ceremonial which commands universal

esteem.... The afternoon tea is now an

important function in western society. In

the delicate clatter of trays and saucers, in

the soft rustle of feminine hospitality, in

the common catechism about cream and

sugar, we know that the worship of tea is

established beyond question... in this single

instance the oriental spirit reigns supreme.

KAKUZO OKAKURA (1862-1913)

Under [tea's] benign influence we have attained... something of the Confucian spirit, a readiness to give and take, an unwillingness to push any argument to its conclusion.... We should, therefore,

regard as public benefactors those who,
during the last couple of centuries,
have made it possible for us
to refine our passions, steady
our nerves, and promote whatever degree
of civilisation we may be supposed
to have reached by
the aid of "a nice cup of tea".

STEPHEN H. TWINING,
FROM THE INTRODUCTION OF
"THE HOUSE OF TWINING"

TAKING TIME FOR TEA

Tea is only a part of the rituals
of the tea ceremony.
Order, beauty, discipline, patience and
courtesy, weave themselves about it.
It is the centre of a heightened perception,
an exercise in concentration,
a moment outside time.

PAM BROWN, b.1928

... let us have a sip of tea.
The afternoon glow is brightening the
bamboos, the fountains are bubbling
with delight, the soughing of the pines
is heard in our kettle. Let us dream
of evanescence, and linger in
the beautiful foolishness of things.

KAKUZO OKAKURA (1862-1913)

A CHANGE OF PACE

Don't hurry. When making tea
you have only time. Let tea be a
refuge, a genuine change of pace.
Brewing your tea is part of drinking
it and drinking it part of your life.
Let the tea gently stimulate you to
reflect on how the smallest part
touches and is touched by
the infinite.

JOEL DAVID AND KARL SCHAPIRA

SPECIAL MOMENTS

"The mere chink of cups and
saucers turns the mind to
happy repose."

GEORGE GISSING (1857-1903)

Sunday morning.
Tea and the newspapers in bed.

PAM BROWN, b.1928

In the hissing of the kettle –
a tranquillizing sound, second only
to the purring of a cat.

AGNES REPPLIER (1855-1950)

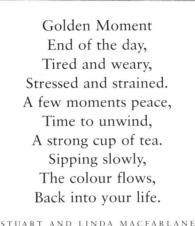

Golden Moment
End of the day,
Tired and weary,
Stressed and strained.
A few moments peace,
Time to unwind,
A strong cup of tea.
Sipping slowly,
The colour flows,
Back into your life.

STUART AND LINDA MACFARLANE

PEACEFUL EVENING

Now stir the fire, and close the shutters fast,
Let fall the curtains, wheel the sofa round,
And while the bubbling and loud-hissing urn
Throws up a steamy column, and the cups
That cheer but not inebriate, wait on each,
So let us welcome peaceful evening in.

WILLIAM COWPER (1731-1800)

Surely every one is aware of the divine pleasures
which attend a wintry fireside: candles at four o'clock,
warm hearthrugs, tea, curtains flowing in ample
draperies to the floor, whilst the wind and rain
are raging audibly without.

THOMAS DE QUINCEY (1785-1859),
FROM "CONFESSIONS OF AN ENGLISH OPIUM-EATER"

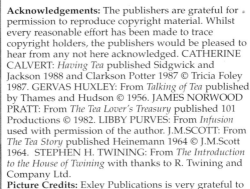
Acknowledgements: The publishers are grateful for permission to reproduce copyright material. Whilst every reasonable effort has been made to trace copyright holders, the publishers would be pleased to hear from any not here acknowledged. CATHERINE CALVERT: *Having Tea* published Sidgwick and Jackson 1988 and Clarkson Potter 1987 © Tricia Foley 1987. GERVAS HUXLEY: From *Talking of Tea* published by Thames and Hudson © 1956. JAMES NORWOOD PRATT: From *The Tea Lover's Treasury* published 101 Productions © 1982. LIBBY PURVES: From *Infusion* used with permission of the author. J.M.SCOTT: From *The Tea Story* published Heinemann 1964 © J.M.Scott 1964. STEPHEN H. TWINING: From *The Introduction to the House of Twining* with thanks to R. Twining and Company Ltd.

Picture Credits: Exley Publications is very grateful to the following individuals and organizations for permission to reproduce their pictures: Artworks (AW), AKG , Bridgeman Art Library (BAL), Fine Art Photographic (FAP), Giraudon (G), Pix, Statens

A Refuge from
the demands of our Lives

People all over the world
take their time in making tea,
as if to acknowledge that making it
is part of drinking it and drinking it
represents a refuge, a moment's respite,
from the demands of our lives.

James Norwood Pratt,
from "The Tea Lovers Treasury"

We are sitting at night in a mountain lodge,
and are boiling tea with water from
a mountain spring. When the fire attacks
the water, we begin to hear a sound similar
to the singing of the wind among pine trees.
We pour the tea into a cup,
and the gentle glow of its light plays
around the place.
The pleasure of such a moment
cannot be shared with vulgar people.

T'U LUNG, FROM "CH'ACHIEH" (c.1592)

THE TEA CEREMONY

The Japanese tea ceremony
requires many years of training and
practice to graduate in the art....
Yet the whole of this art, as to detail,
signifies no more than the making and
serving of a cup of tea. However, it is a
real art – a most exquisite art.

LAFCADIO HEARN (1850-1904)

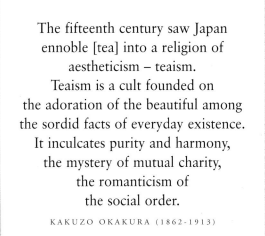

The fifteenth century saw Japan
ennoble [tea] into a religion of
aestheticism – teaism.
Teaism is a cult founded on
the adoration of the beautiful among
the sordid facts of everyday existence.
It inculcates purity and harmony,
the mystery of mutual charity,
the romanticism of
the social order.

KAKUZO OKAKURA (1862-1913)

Van Strydonck

TEA'S GIFT TO THE WORLD

... tea's great contribution
to the world lies outside
commerce or art or politics.
Its gift is the benign influence
that it exercises on the social
life of mankind. It is not only
in Japan that tea drinking has
been elevated to an aesthetic
cult, tea everywhere helps to
make the world a friendlier
and a kindlier place of
sojourn for men and women.

GERVAS HUXLEY,
FROM "TALKING OF TEA"

THE JAPANESE TEA CEREMONY

Tea with us became more than an
idealization of the form of drinking; it is
a religion of the art of life.
The beverage grew to be an excuse for
the worship of purity and refinement,
a sacred function at which the host and
guest joined to produce for that occasion
the utmost beatitude of the mundane.
The tearoom was an oasis in the dreary
waste of existence where weary travellers
could meet to drink from the common
spring of art-appreciation.
The ceremony was an improvised drama